TURN-OF-THE-CENTURY POSTERS
Coloring Book

38 Designs Rendered
for Coloring by
ED SIBBETT, Jr.

Dover Publications, Inc.
New York

Published in Canada by General Publishing Company, Ltd., 30 Lesmill Road, Don Mills, Toronto, Ontario.
Published in the United Kingdom by Constable and Company, Ltd., 10 Orange Street, London WC2H 7EG.

Turn-of-the-Century Posters Coloring Book is a new work, first published by Dover Publications, Inc., in 1978.

DOVER *Pictorial Archive* SERIES

Turn-of-the-Century Posters Coloring Book belongs to the Dover Pictorial Archive Series. Up to four illustrations from this book may be used on any one project or in any single publication, free and without special permission. Wherever possible please include a credit line indicating the title of this book, artist and publisher. Please address the publisher for permission to make more extensive use of illustrations than that authorized above.
The republication of this book in whole is prohibited.

International Standard Book Number: 0-486-23705-2

Manufactured in the United States of America
Dover Publications, Inc.
180 Varick Street
New York, N.Y. 10014

PUBLISHER'S NOTE

The spread of lithography in the earlier nineteenth century created the poster industry as we know it today, and many handsome posters were produced in that period. In general, however, the designers were anonymous employees of the printing establishments and their work was considered a craft.

Despite such brilliant harbingers as Jules Chéret, whose inventive work began in the 1850s, it was not until the 1890s that the "poster revolution" arrived, ushering in the golden age of the poster. Throughout the Western world, with the chief impetus coming from France, posters were designed by famous artists, avidly collected and exhibited in galleries. Their brilliant colors enlivened the streets of the world's great cities.

To give the readers an opportunity to recreate these colors (17 of the original posters are reproduced on the covers) or to conceive their own bold color schemes, the artist Ed Sibbett, Jr., has rendered 38 outstanding works from this golden age. Included along with the pioneer Chéret are such other great French illustrators as Toulouse-Lautrec, Steinlen and Boutet de Monvel. America is well represented by Edward Penfield, Maxfield Parrish, Louis Rhead, the distinguished woman artist Alice Russell Glenny and Will W. Denslow, the famous illustrator of *The Wizard of Oz*.

Specially significant inclusions in this book are a number of posters in the purest Art Nouveau style, which was also a product of the same creative decade. Among the Art Nouveau practitioners represented here are Eugène Grasset, one of the chief theoreticians of the movement as well as an incomparable artist; Will Bradley, who acclimatized the style in America; and Alphonse Marie Mucha, archpriest of Art Nouveau and one of the greatest poster artists of all time. Mucha's poster for Bernhardt's *Medea* is printed, on one side of the sheet only, as the centerfold of this book—an ideal piece for framing after it has been colored.

LIST OF POSTERS

EXPOSITION

DE

TABLEAUX & DESSINS DE A. WILLETTE

Ouverture
LE
15 FÉVRIER

34, Rue de Provence

9

Lait pur de la Vingeanne
Stérilisé

Guillot frères
Montigny sur Vingeanne
Côte d'Or

13

WHEN HEARTS
ARE TRUMPS
BY TOM HALL

LA PETITE POUCETTE

MUSIQUE DE RAOUL PUGNO

L'ERMITAGE

18

LEÇONS DE VIOLON DE VIOLONCELLE & DE SOLFÈGE (PRIX MODÉRÉS) D'ACCOMPAGNEMENT S'ADRESSER 22, rue Denfert-Rochereau

HARPER'S
MAY

A NEW LIFE OF NAPOLEON
MAGNIFICENTLY ILLUSTRATED

IS NOW BEGINNING IN
THE CENTURY MAGAZINE

THE CENTURY

Midsummer.
Holiday Number.
August.

WOMENS EDITION (BUFFALO) COURIER

THE SUN

·Gives·best·results·

ELITE

MARCH

HARPER'S

OCTOBER

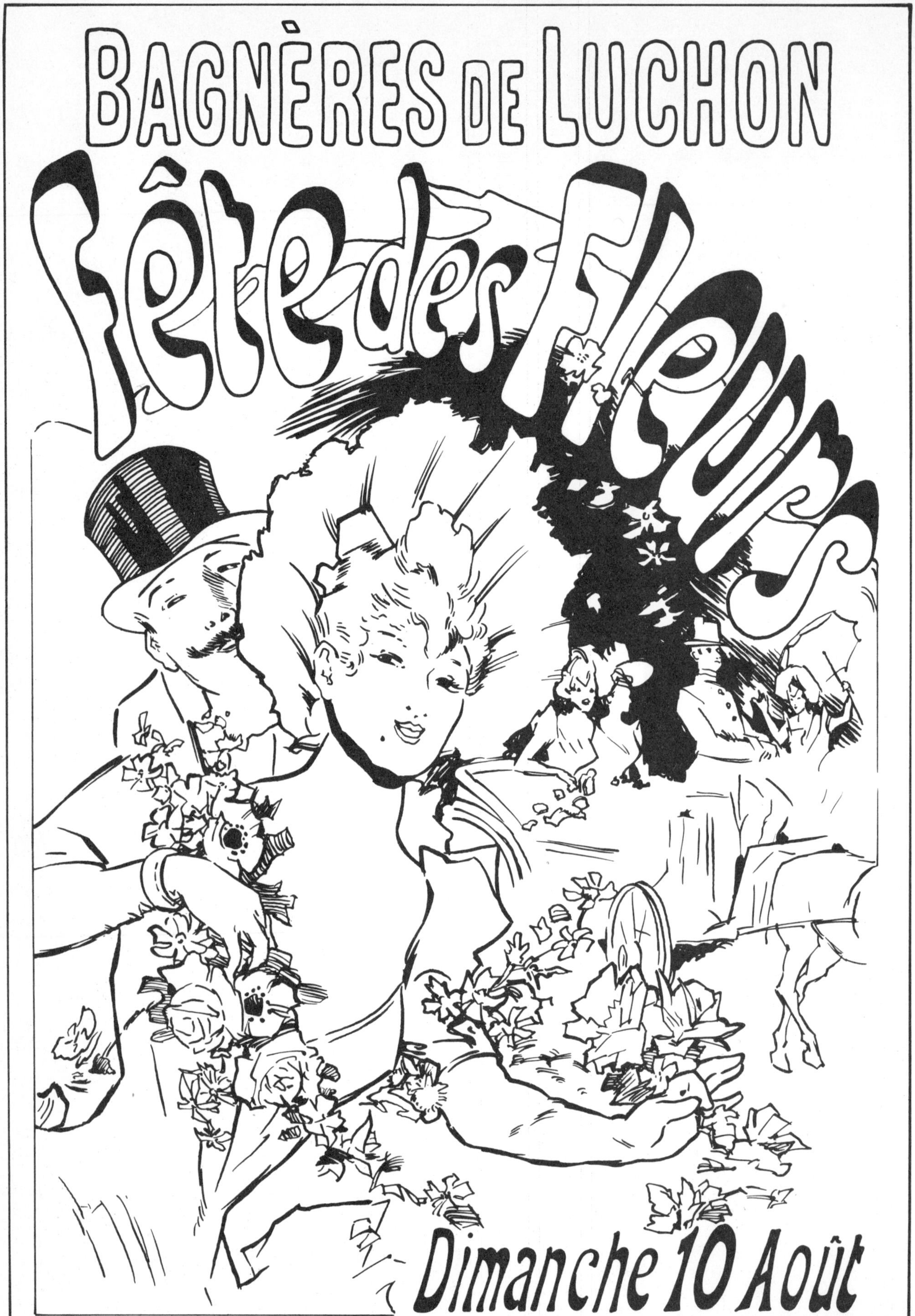
BAGNÈRES DE LUCHON
Fête des Fleurs
Dimanche 10 Août

DOVER COLORING BOOKS

Paperbound unless otherwise indicated. Prices subject to change without notice. Available at your book dealer or write for free catalogues to Dept. Mathematics, Dover Publications, Inc., 180 Varick Street, New York, N.Y. 10014. Please indicate field of interest. Each year Dover publishes over 200 books on fine art, music, crafts and needlework, antiques, languages, literature, children's books, chess, cookery, nature, anthropology, science, mathematics, and other areas.

Manufactured in the U.S.A.